Map Legend

Borders

Country border
Natural Park border
Military/restricted area

Fence

Gate

Roads & Paths

Surfaced roads
Dirt roads & tracks

Walking trails
Restricted/guided trails
Obligatory walking direction
Major hiking/trekking routes
Downhill skiing routes & lifts

Natural Terrain

Lakes, ponds
Rivers; streams
Waterfalls
Wetland
Wood
Scrub
Heath
Meadow; grass
Sand; beach
Glacier
Crevasse
Cliffs; rocks; arete
Scree; shingle
Viewpoint
Cave entrance

Man-made Features

Farmland

Orchard
Power line
Railroad
Pipeline

Quarry
Monument, tourist attraction
Cemetery

Amenities

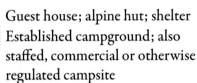

Guardería Coirón   R   Rangers post
Pol   Police station; border control
Tourist information
Hotel, hostel
Guest house; alpine hut; shelter

Established campground; also
staffed, commercial or otherwise
regulated campsite

Closed campsite

Hospital
Post office
Playground

Transportation & Transport Amenities

Car parking
Bus station/hub
Bus stop
Ferry & cruise ship routes

Airport

Food

Cafe, restaurant, bakery
Grocery store; supermarket

All Elevations are in Meters

Mercator Projection

Sergio Mazitto Tourist Topo Maps

Available from
Amazon.com and other retailers

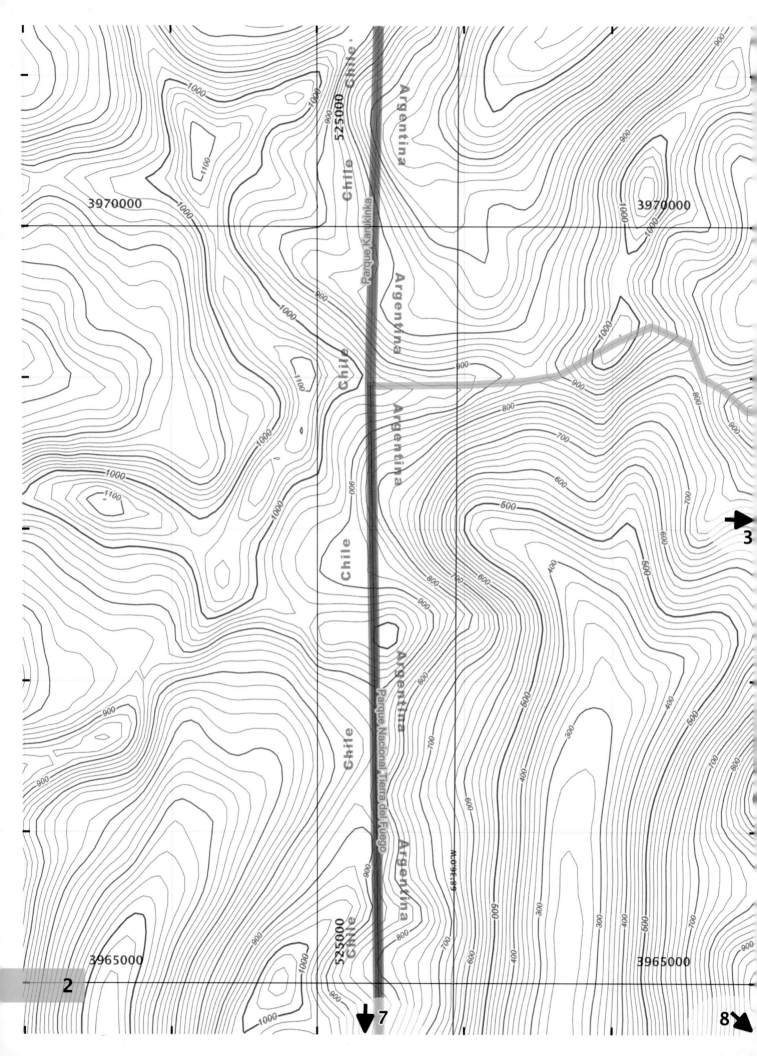

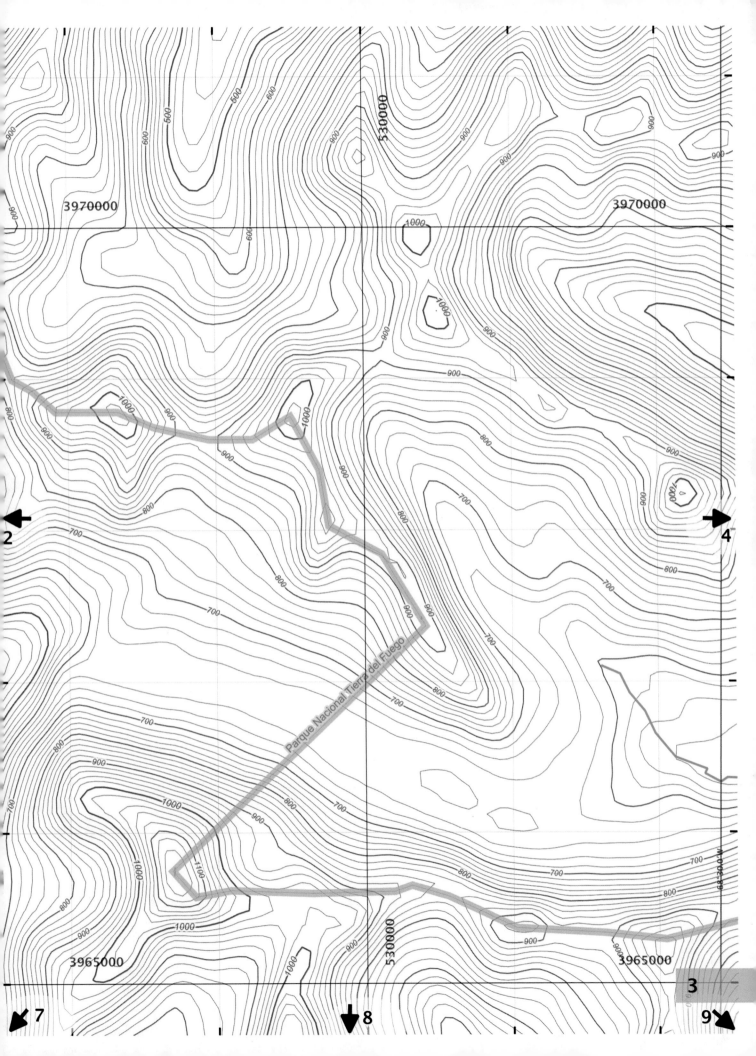

3970000

530000

3970000

500
600
900
900
900
900
1000
1000
900
900
900
900
900

1000

1000
900
900
800
800
1000
800
800
900
800
700
900
900
900
700
800
900
700
800
800
800
900
800

Parque Nacional Tierra del Fuego

700
700
800
900
700
700
700
700
800
800
800
1000
900
900
800
800
700
900
1100
700
700
1000
1000
800
900
800

3965000

530000

3965000

2

4

7

8

9

3

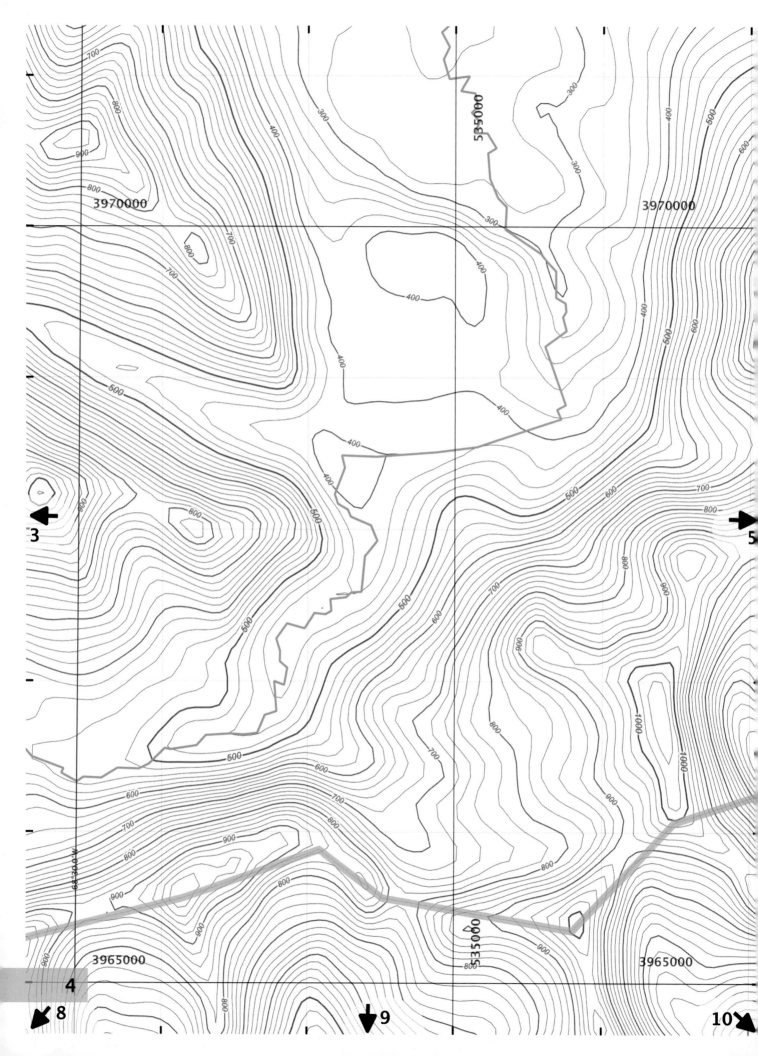

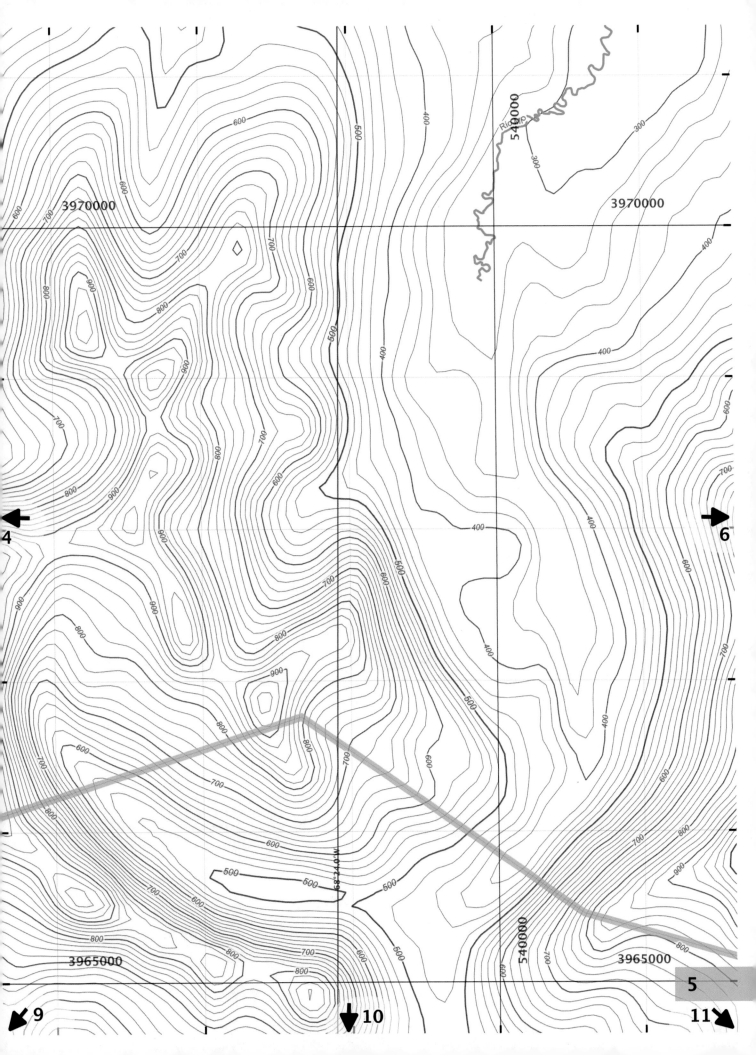

3970000

3970000

Rio DP

540000

4

6

3965000

540000

3965000

5

9

10

11

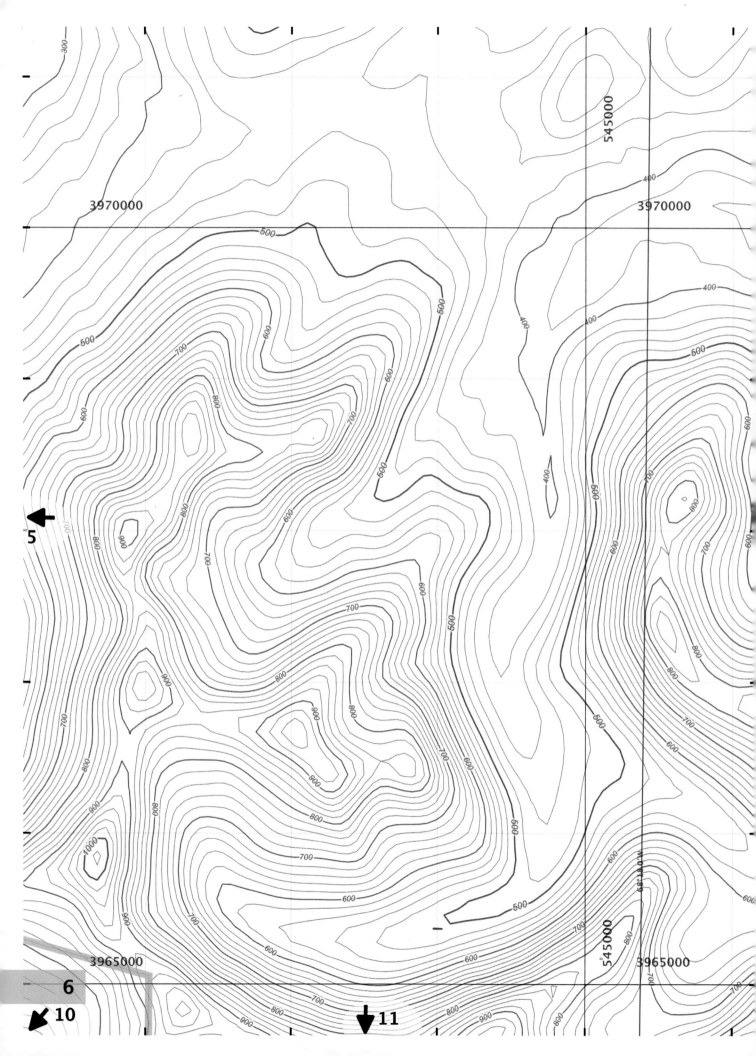

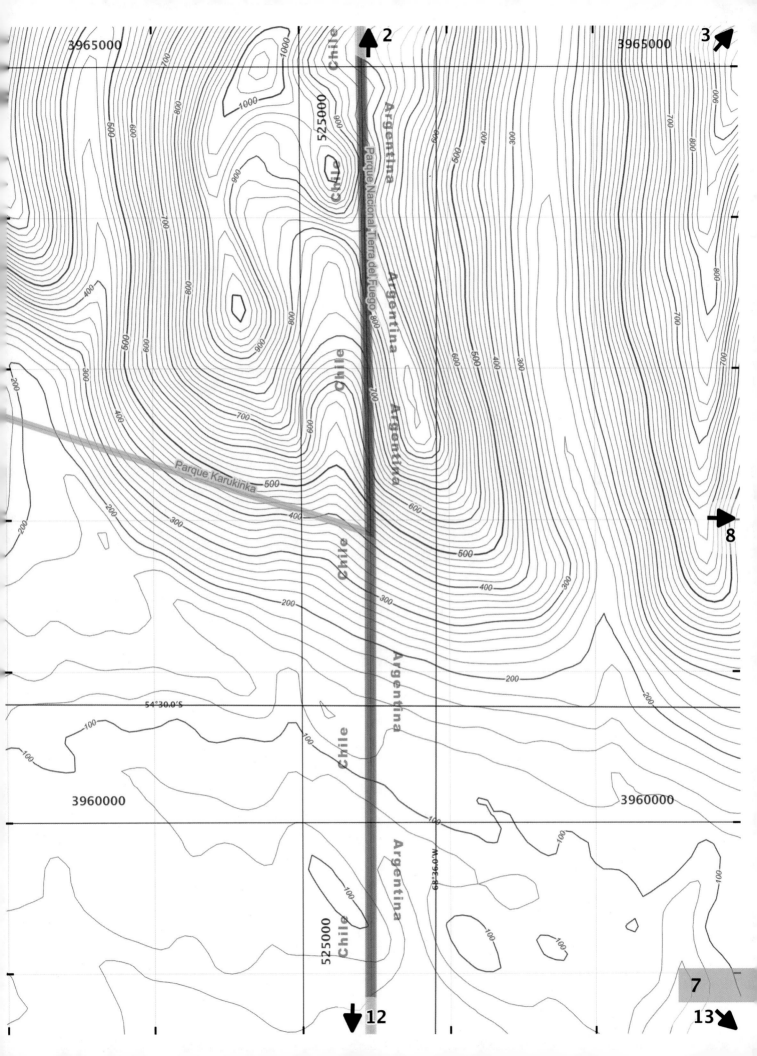

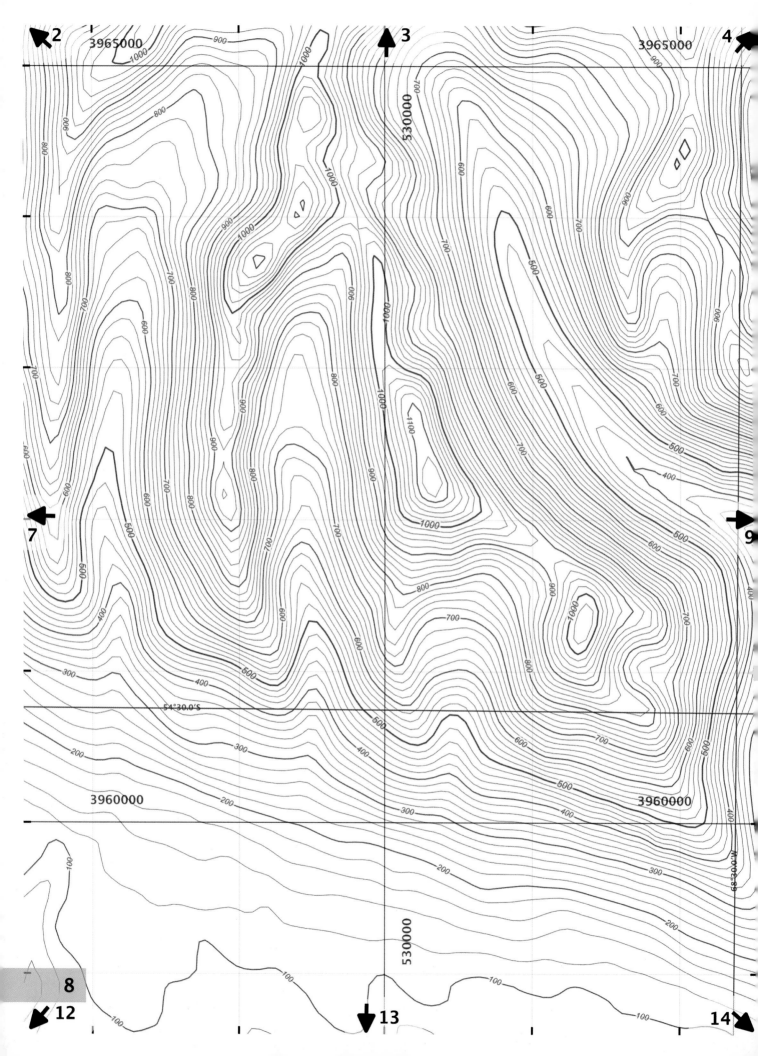

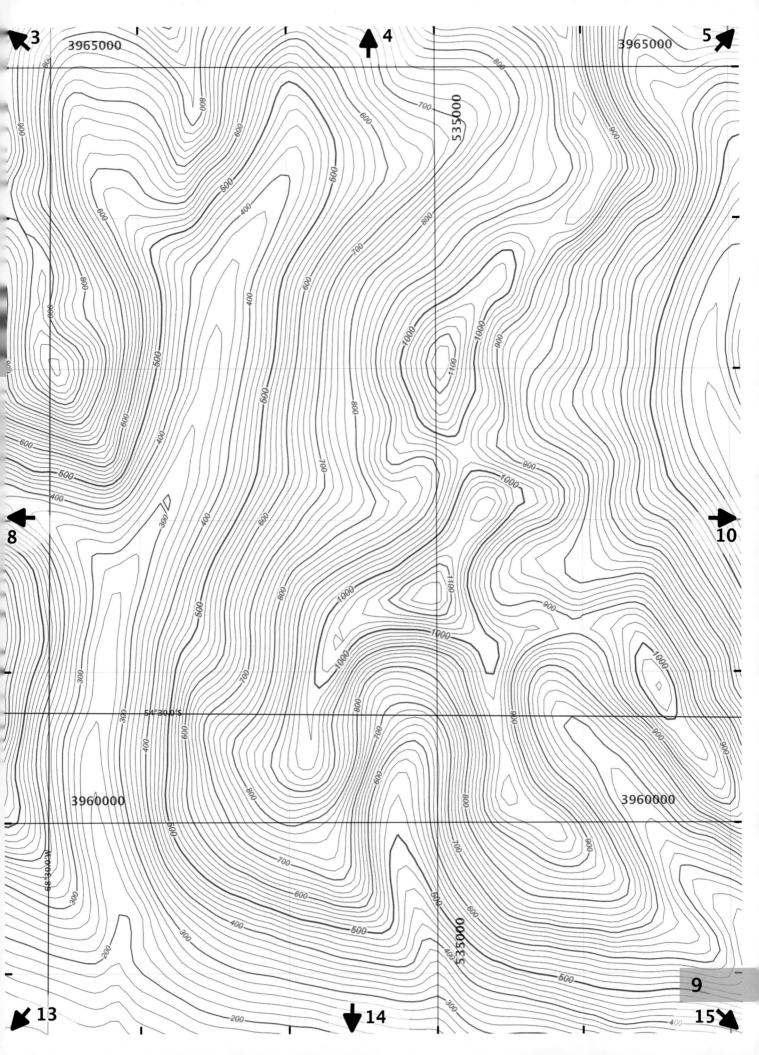

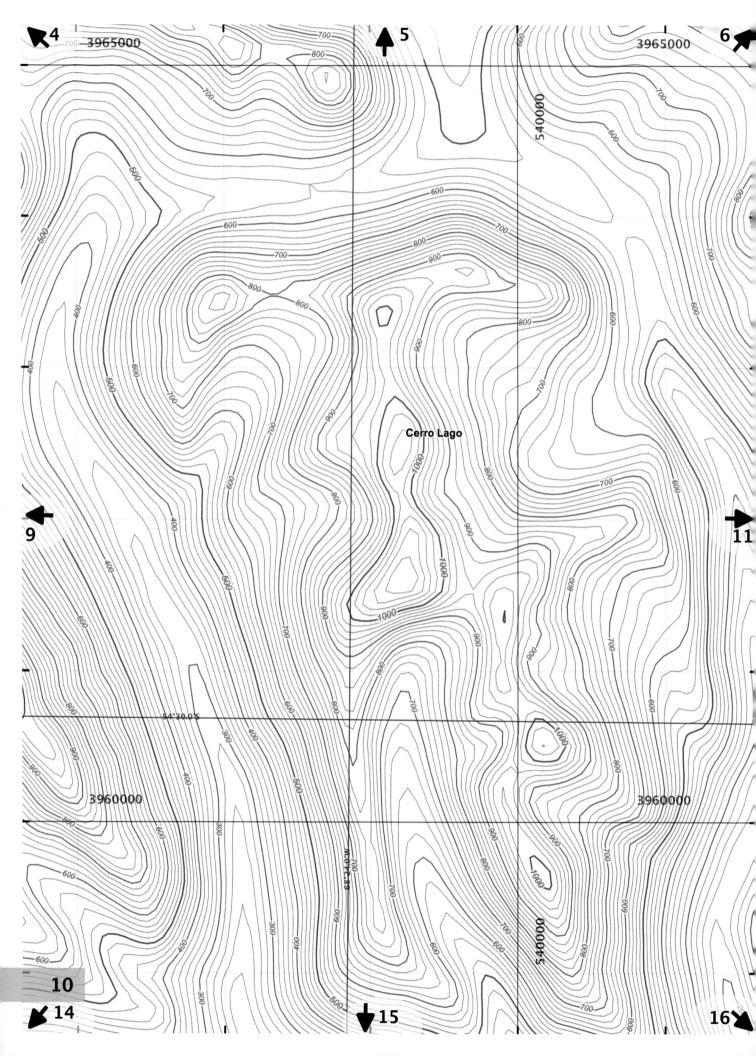

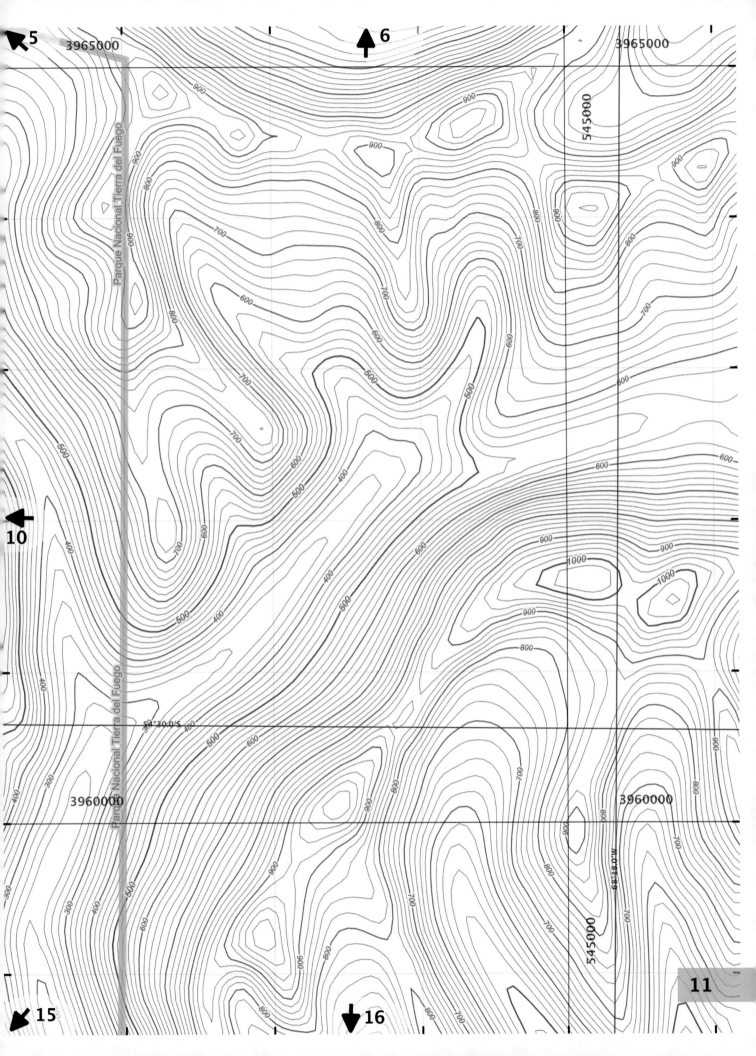

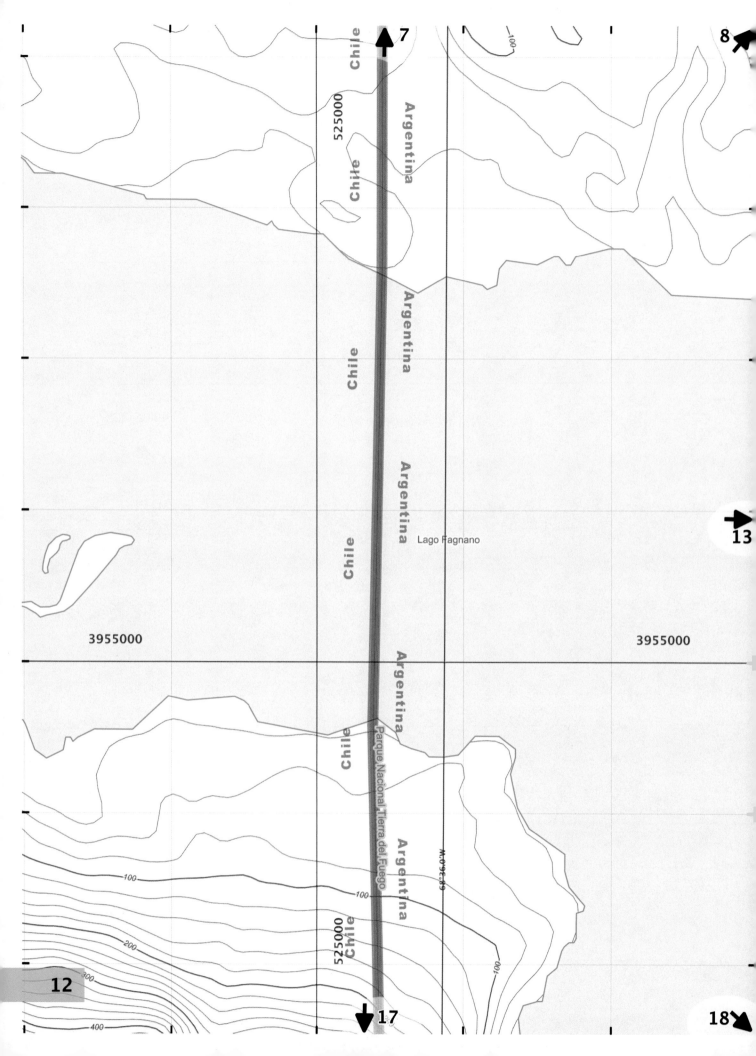

Chile

Chile

525000

Argentina

Chile

Argentina

Chile

Argentina

Chile

Lago Fagnano

13

3955000

3955000

Argentina

Chile

Parque Nacional Tierra del Fuego

Argentina

100

100

525000
Chile

200

300

400

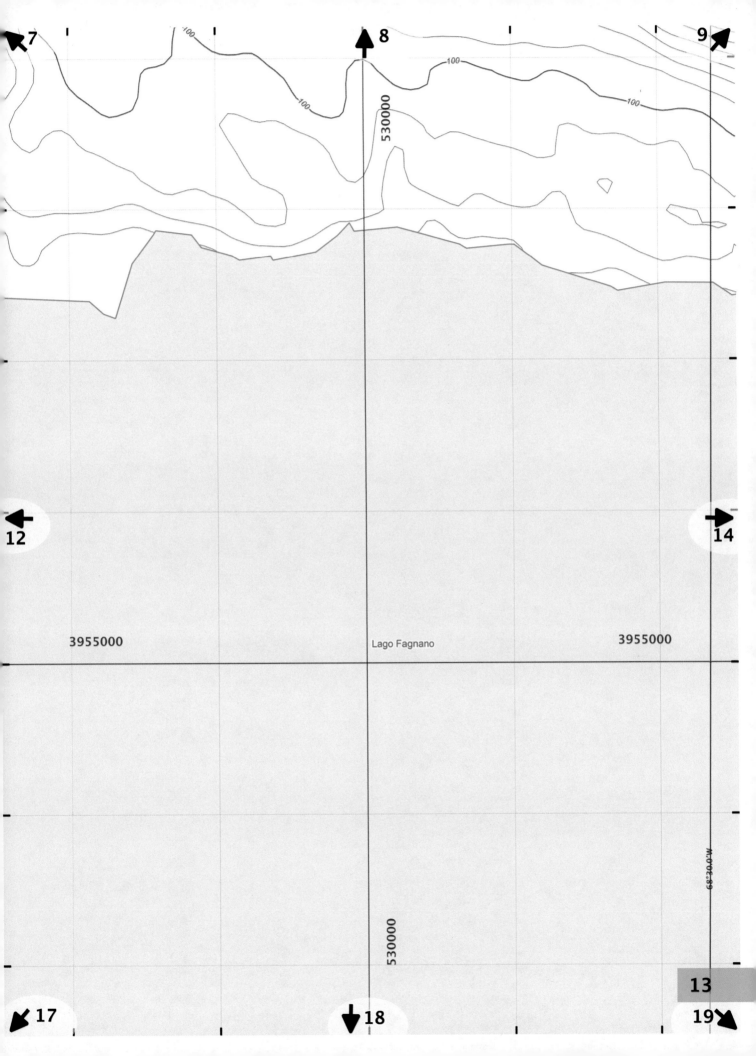

7

8

530000

9

100

100

100

100

100

12

14

3955000

Lago Fagnano

3955000

530000

68.300,00 W.

13

17

18

19

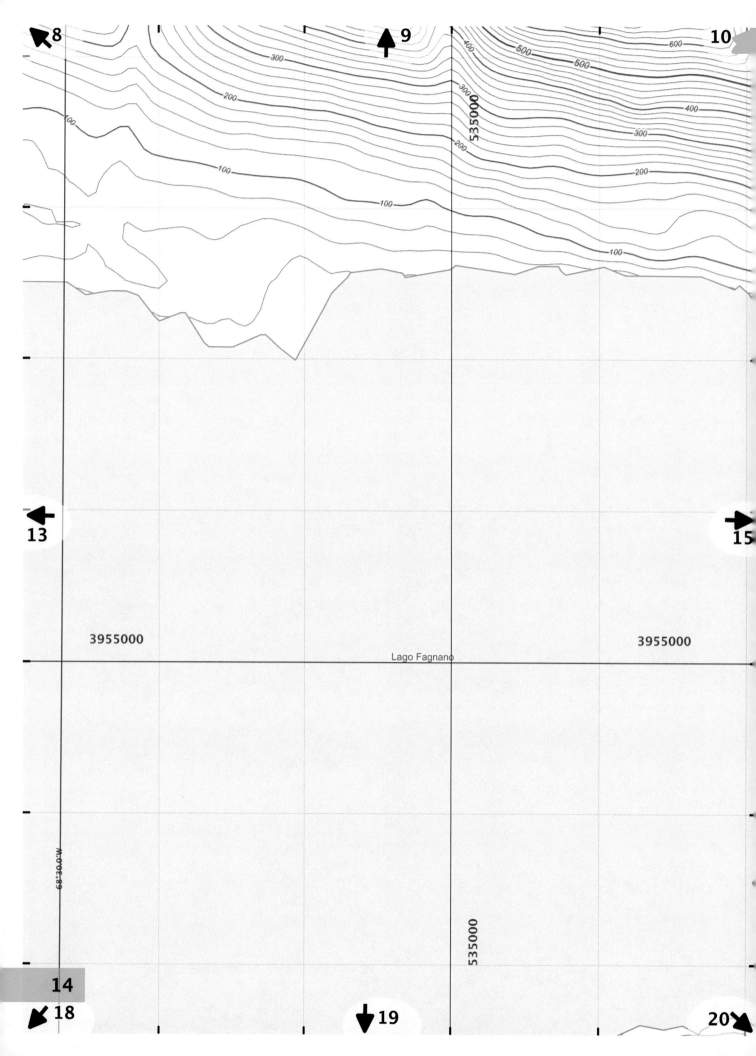

8

9

10

300

200

400

500

600

400

500

535000

300

300

200

200

100

100

100

100

13

15

3955000

3955000

Lago Fagnano

68°30'W

535000

14

18

19

535000

20

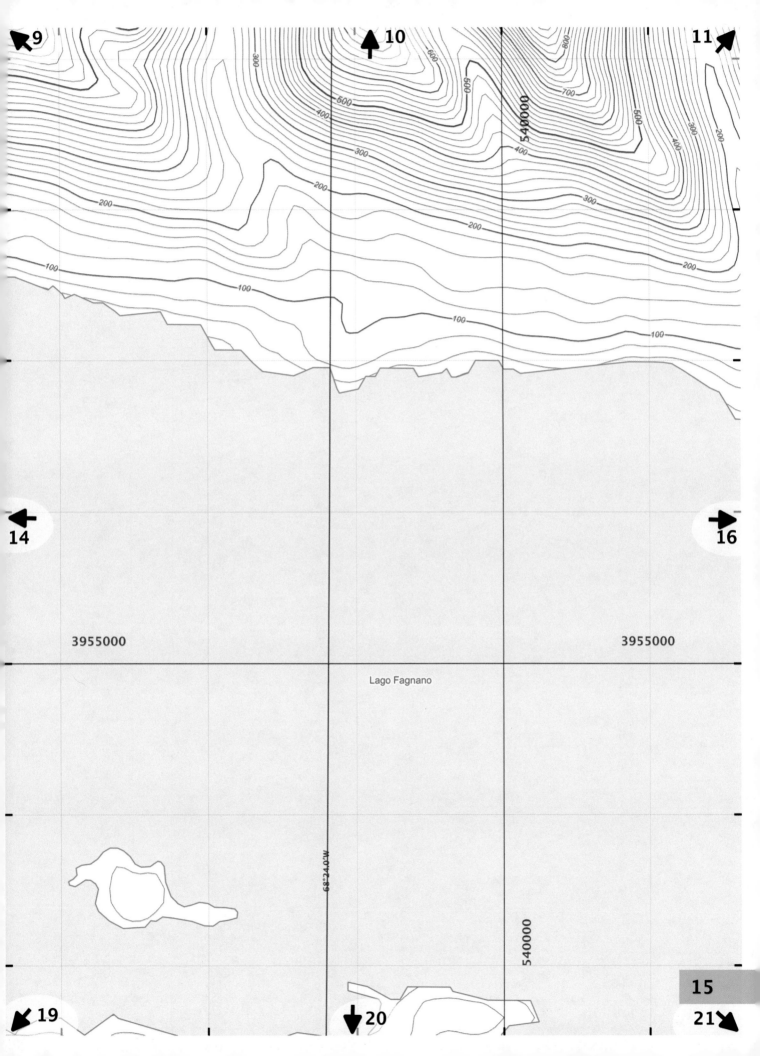

9

10

11

14

16

19

20

15

21

300

600

500

400

700

540000

600

300

400

200

200

300

200

200

100

100

200

100

100

100

100

3955000

3955000

Lago Fagnano

684240 m.

540000

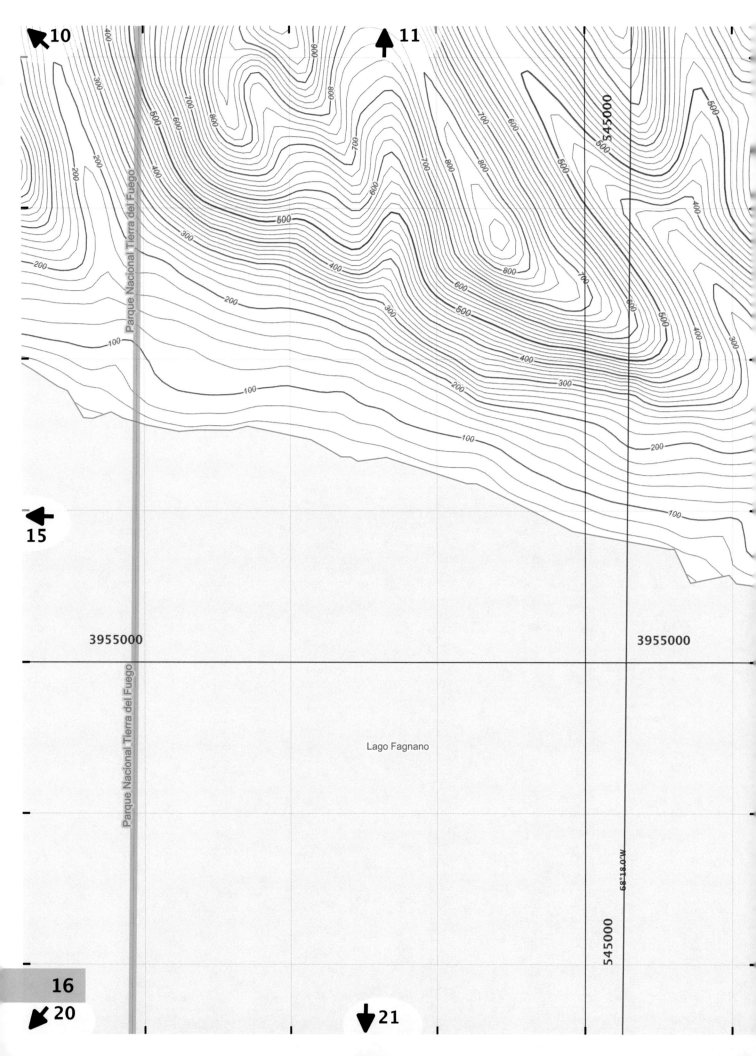

10

11

15

3955000

3955000

545000

68°18.0'W

545000

Parque Nacional Tierra del Fuego

Parque Nacional Tierra del Fuego

Lago Fagnano

16

20

21

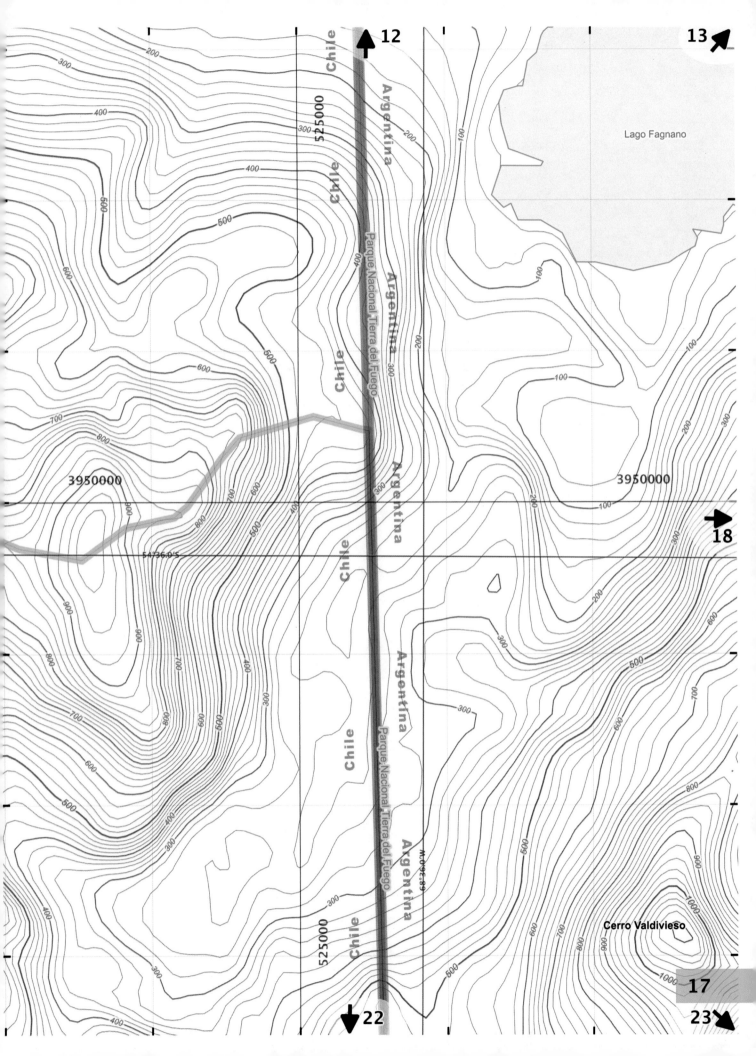

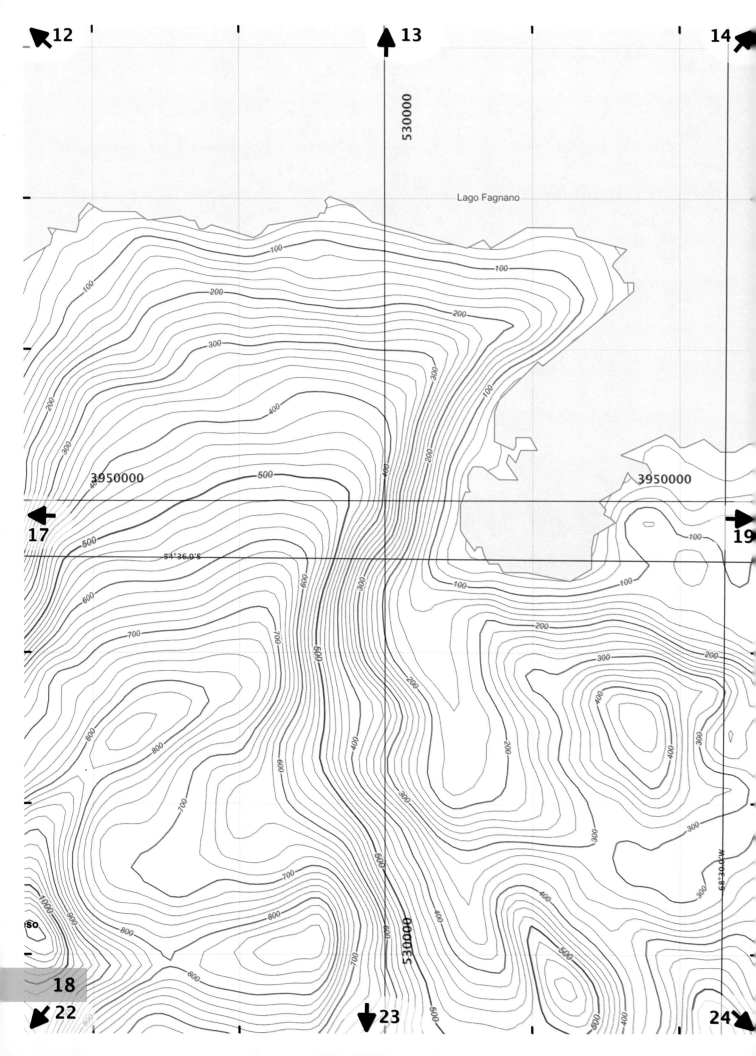

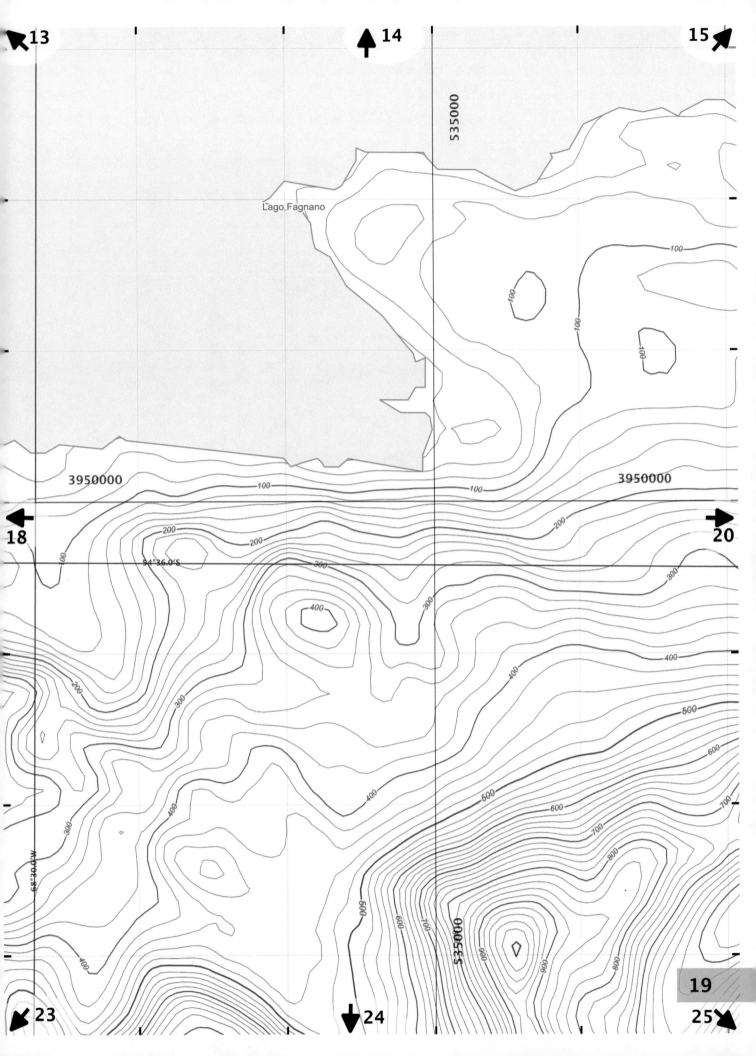

13

14

15

535000

Lago Fagnano

100

100

100

100

3950000

100

100

3950000

18

200

200

200

100

200

20

54°36.0'S

300

300

300

400

300

300

300

400

200

300

400

500

200

400

400

600

300

500

500

600

700

400

400

500

600

700

300

600

800

68°30.0'W

500

700

900

800

400

600

700

533000

900

800

19

23

24

25

14

15

16

540000

Lago Fagnano

100

100

100

100

100

100

100

200

3950000

3950000

200

200

200

19

21

54°36.0'S

300

300

300

300

300

400

500

600

300

500

400

700

500

300

68°24.0'W

400

600

600

700

800

540000

600

600

900

800

540000

800

20

24

25

26

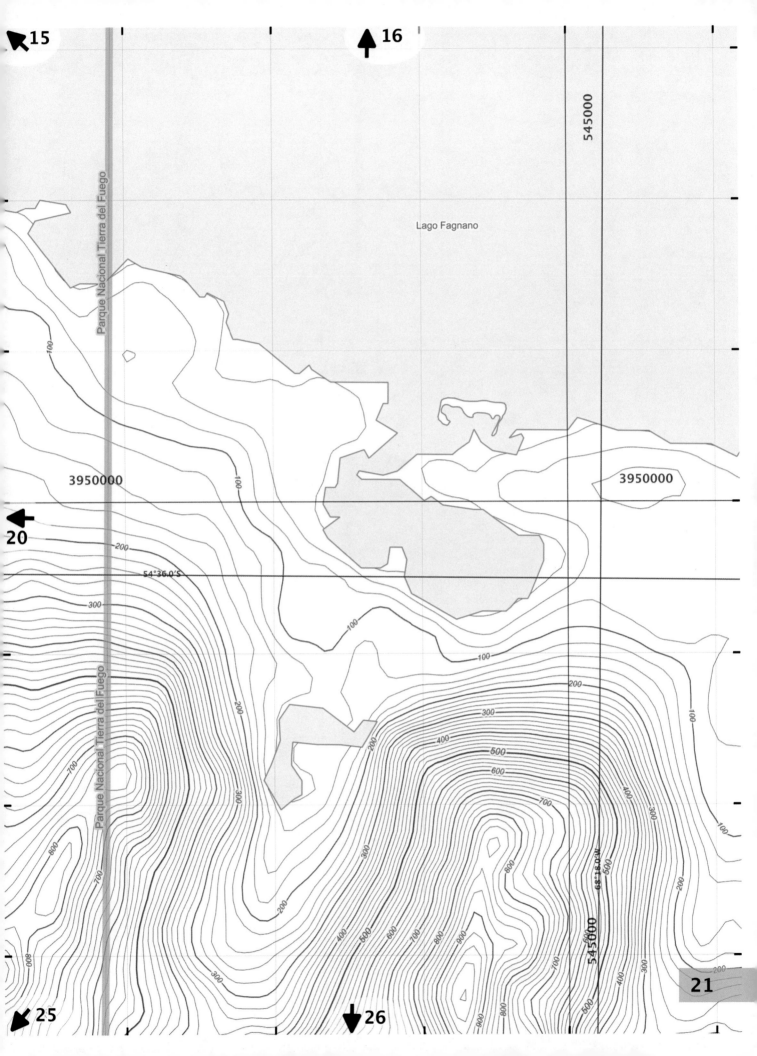

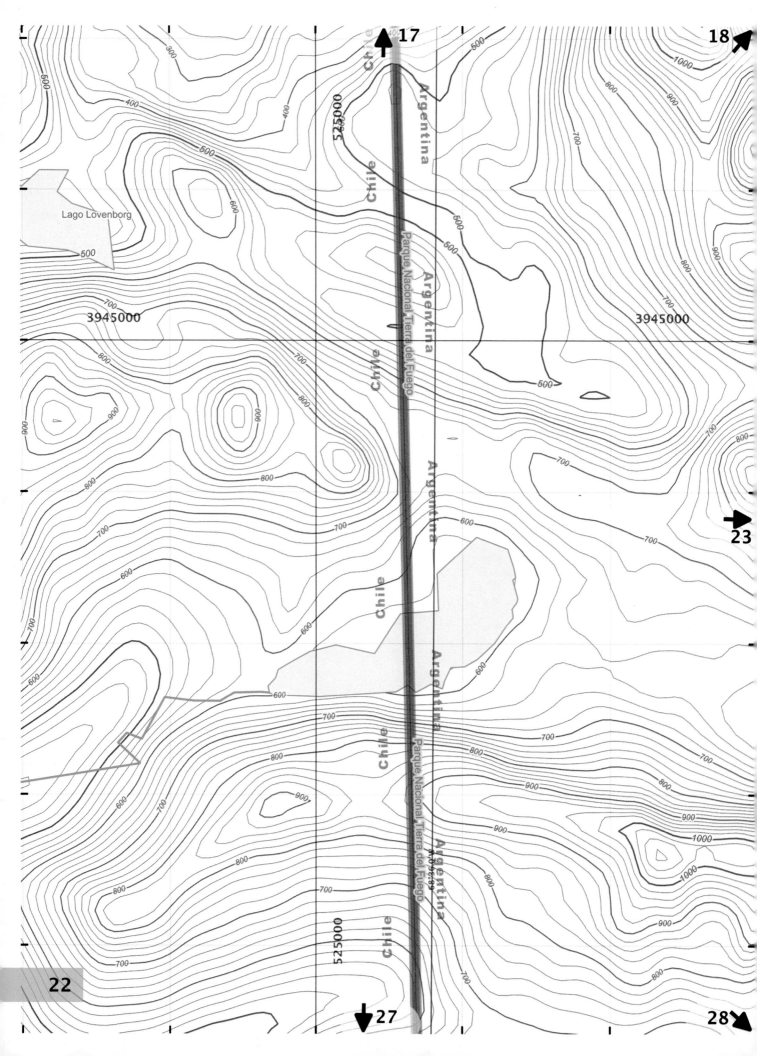

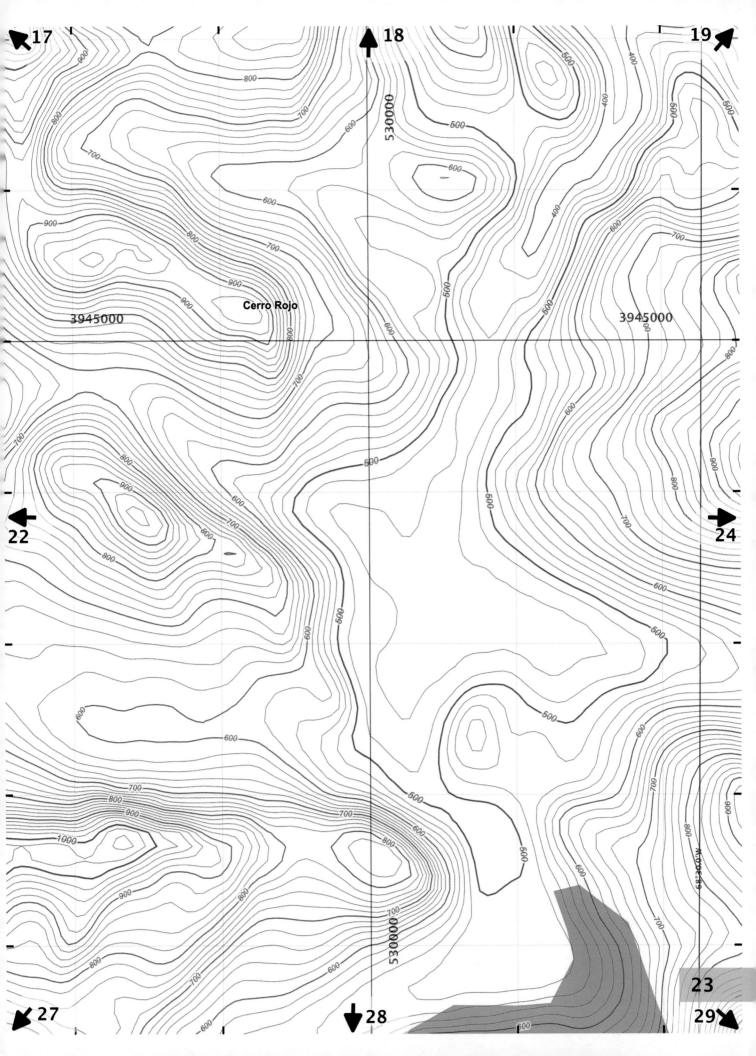

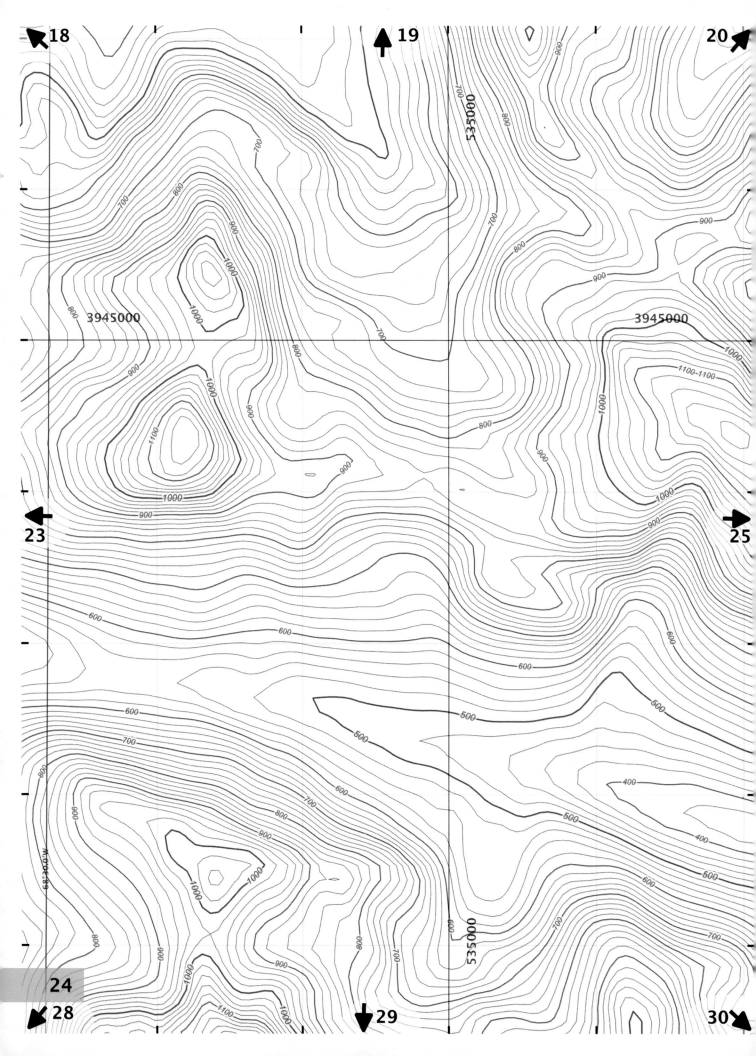

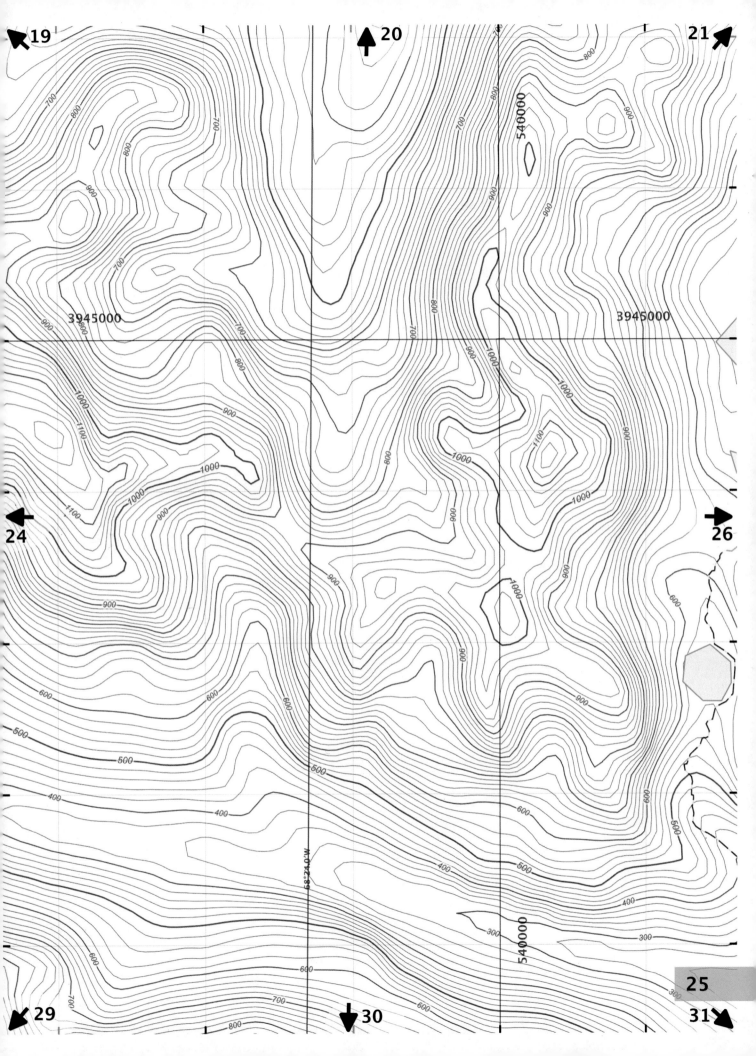

19

20

21

540000

3945000

3945000

24

26

25

29

30

31

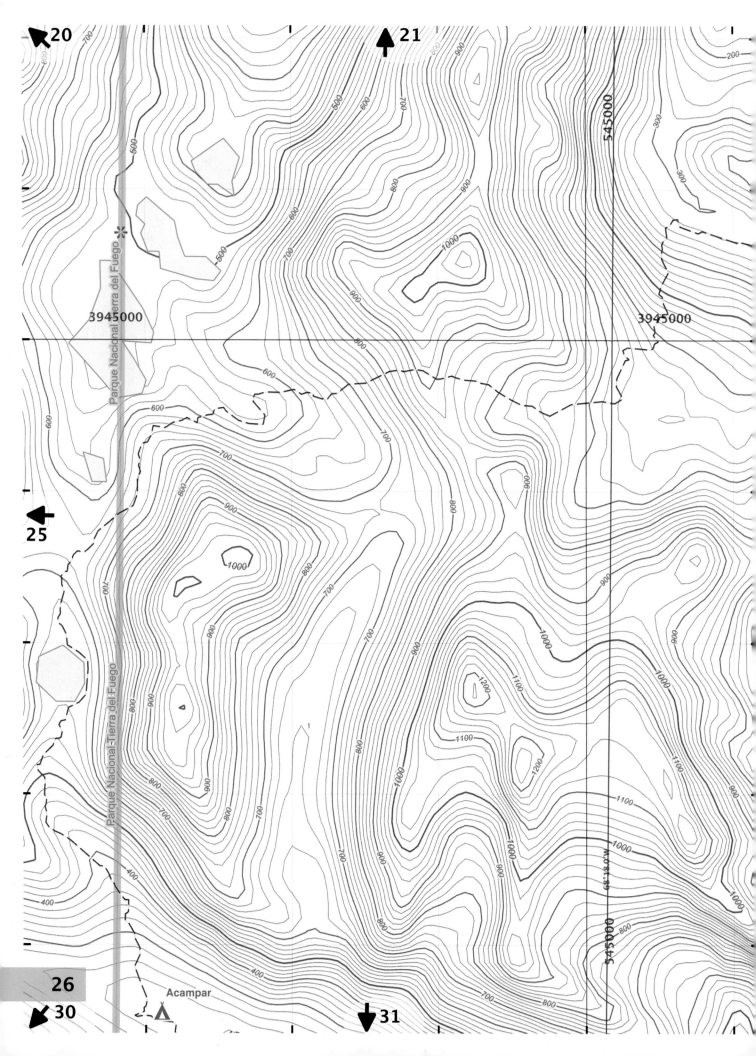

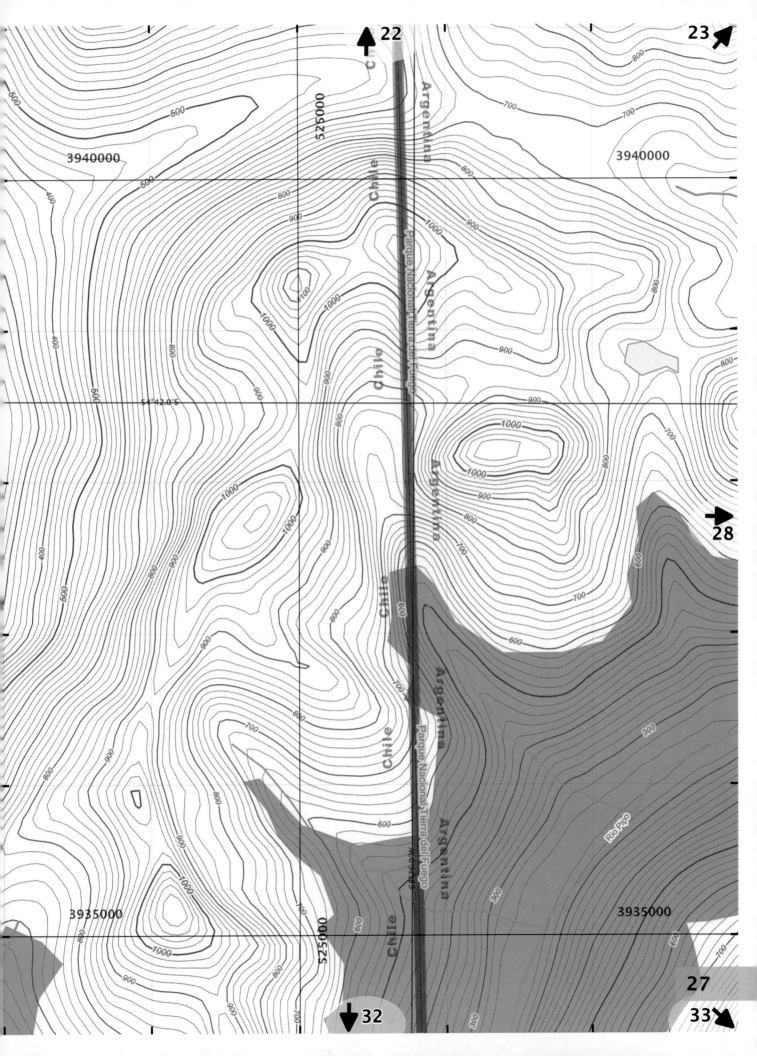

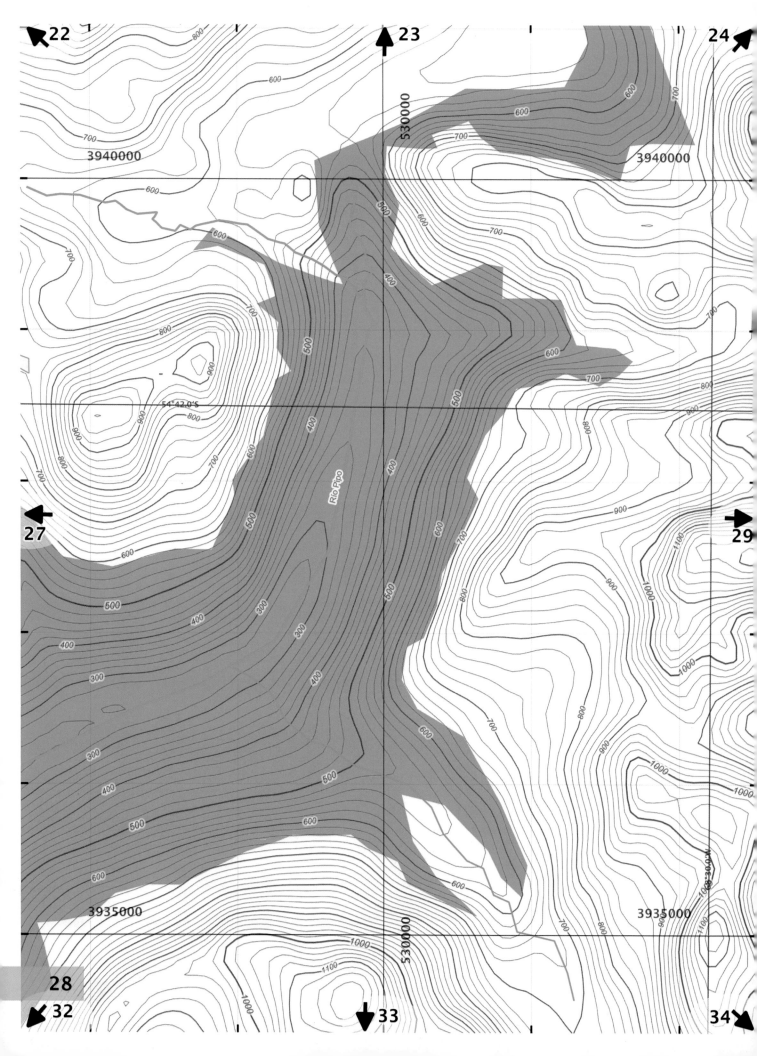

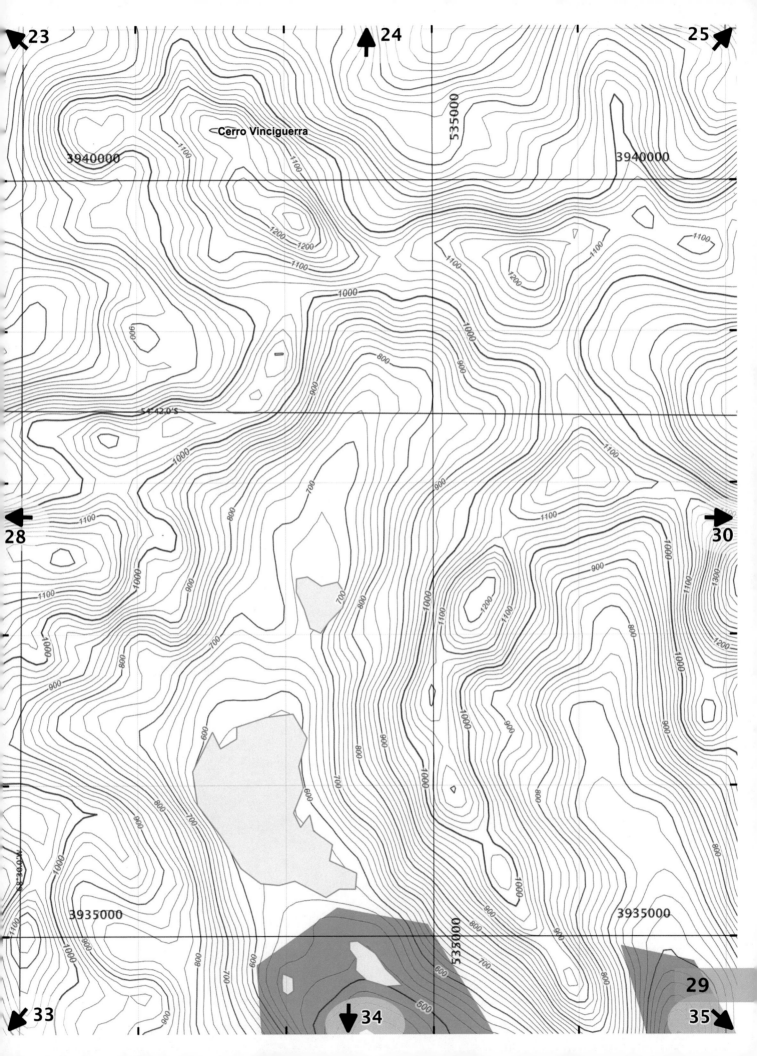

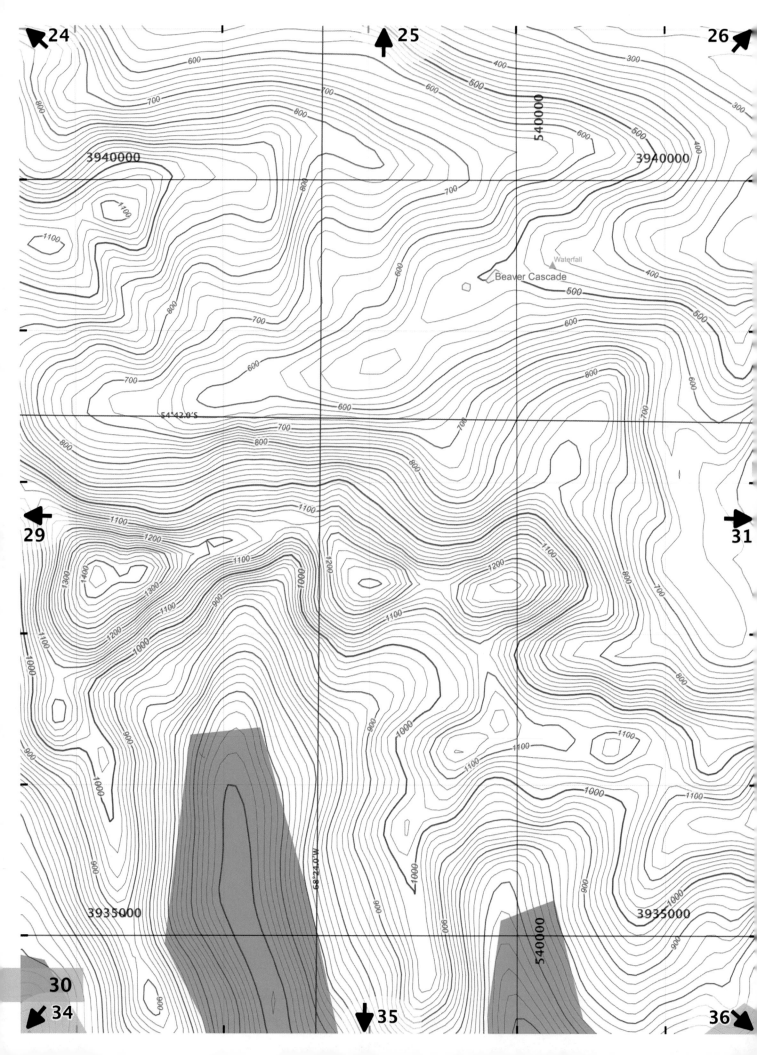

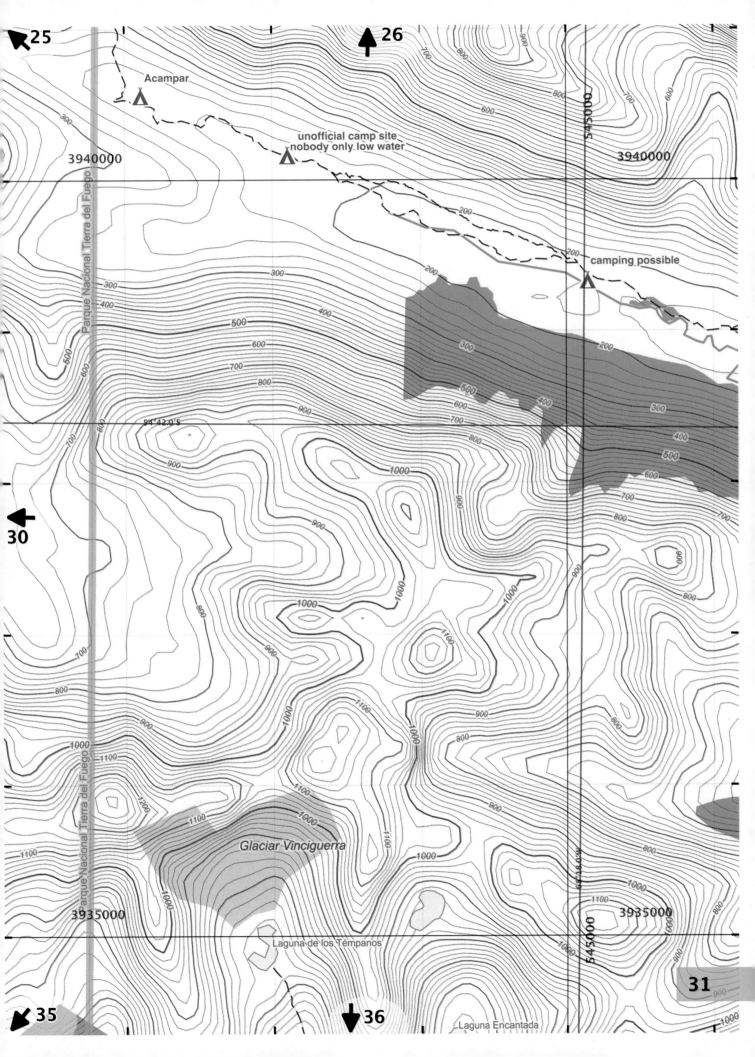

25

26

Acampar

unofficial camp site
nobody only low water

camping possible

3940000

545000

3940000

300

200

300

400

500

600

700

800

900

54°42.0'S

30

Parque Nacional Tierra del Fuego

Glaciar Vinciguerra

3935000

545000

3935000

Laguna de los Témpanos

35

36

31

Laguna Encantada

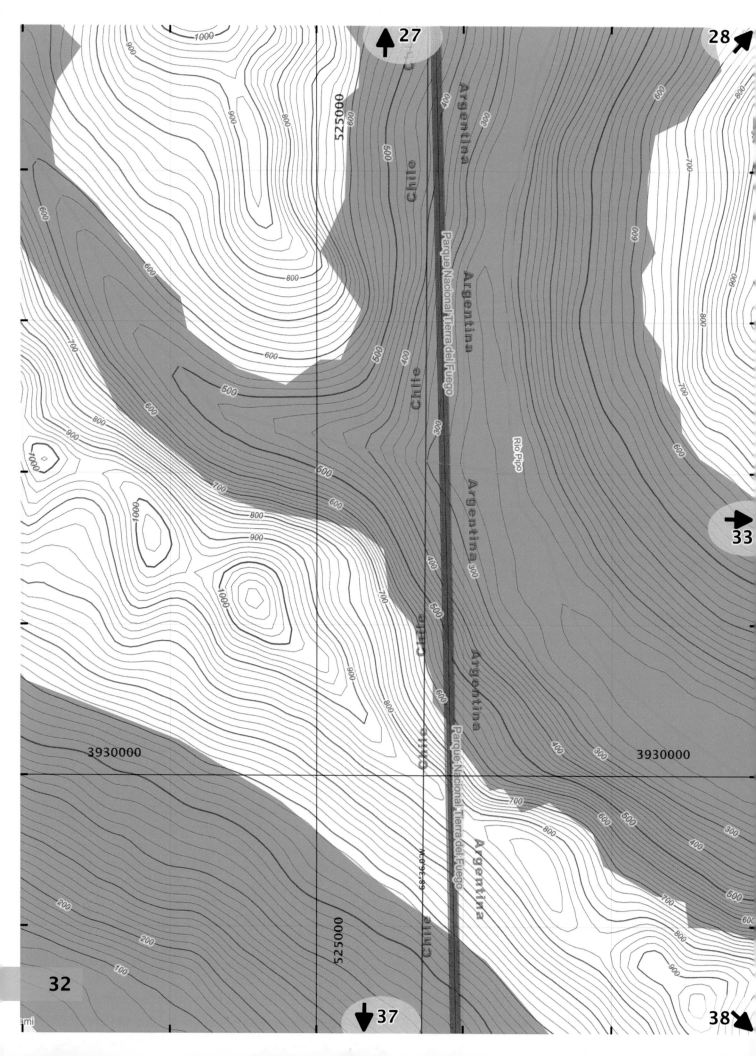

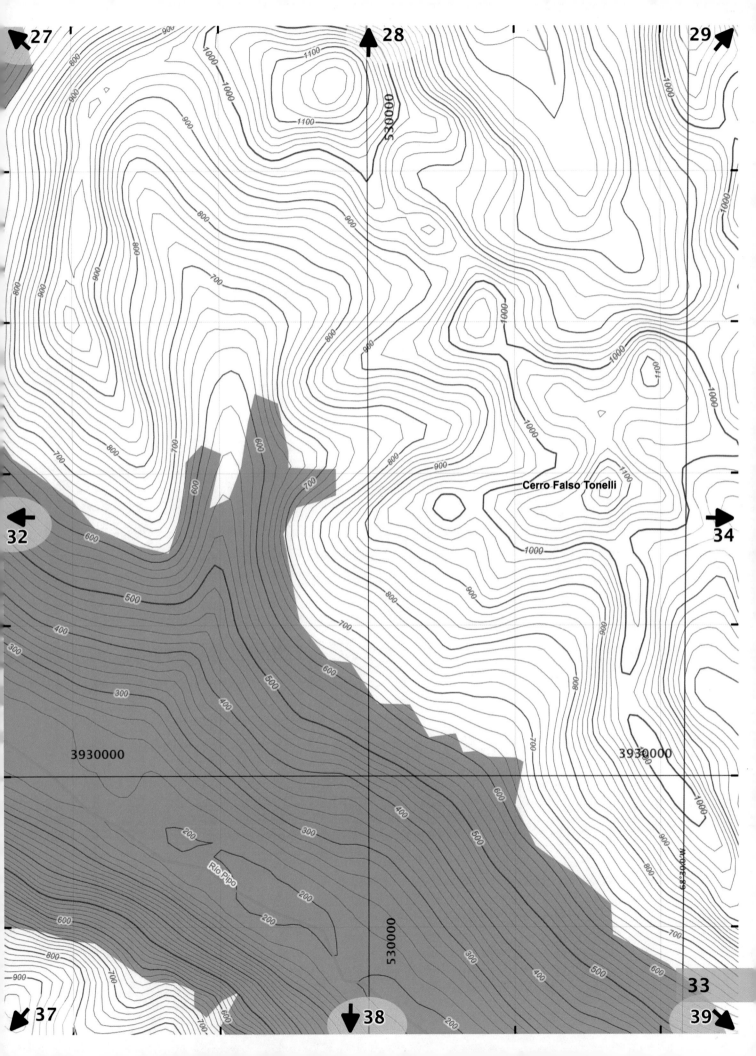

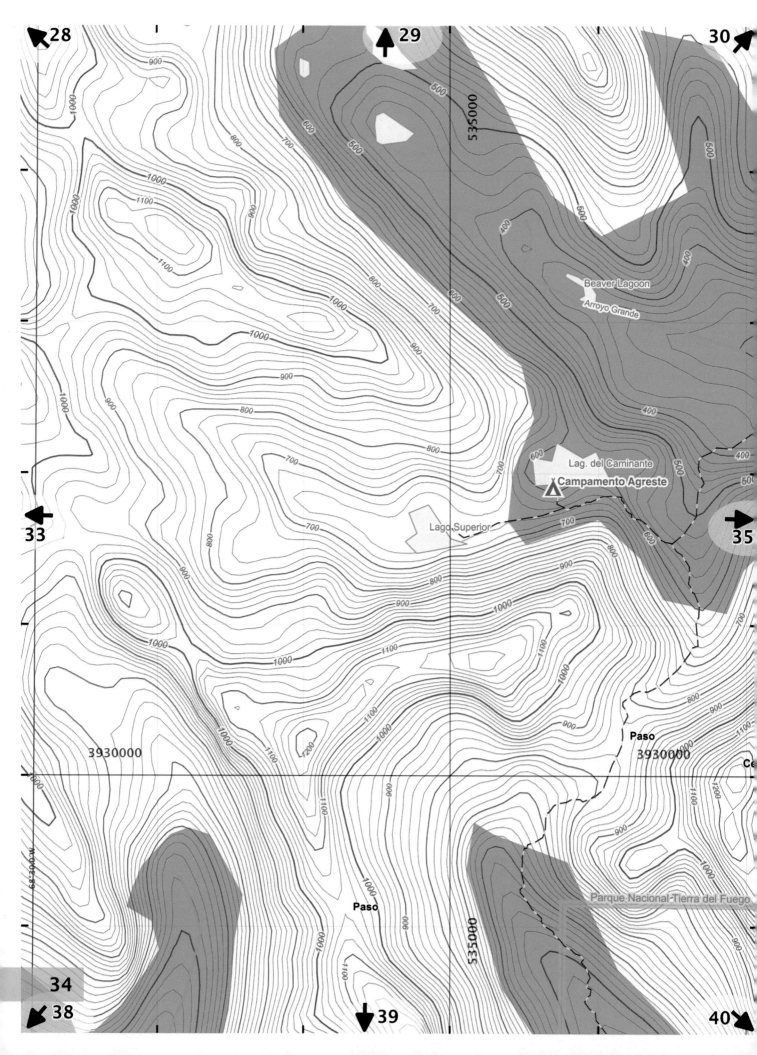

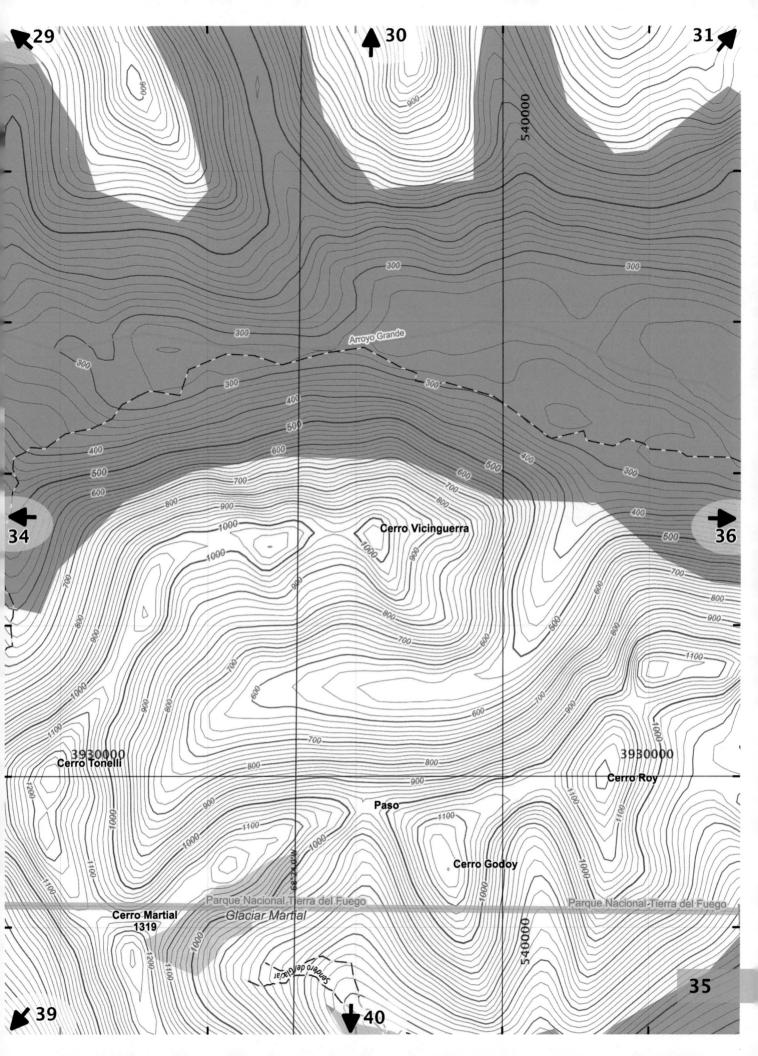

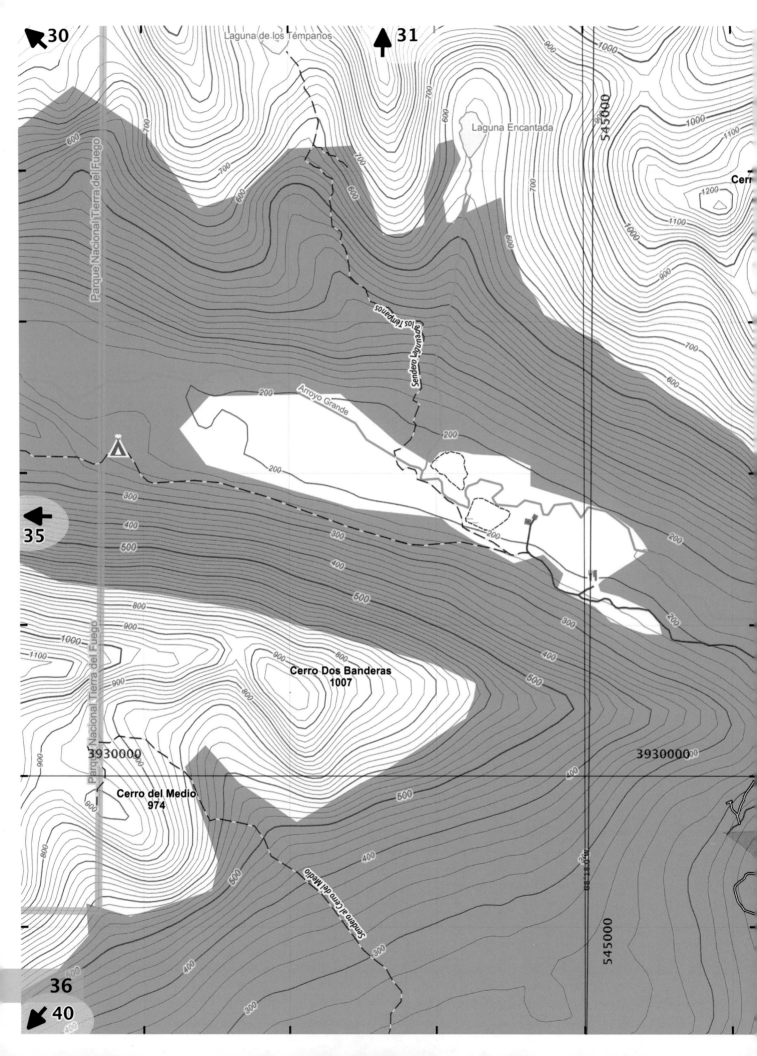

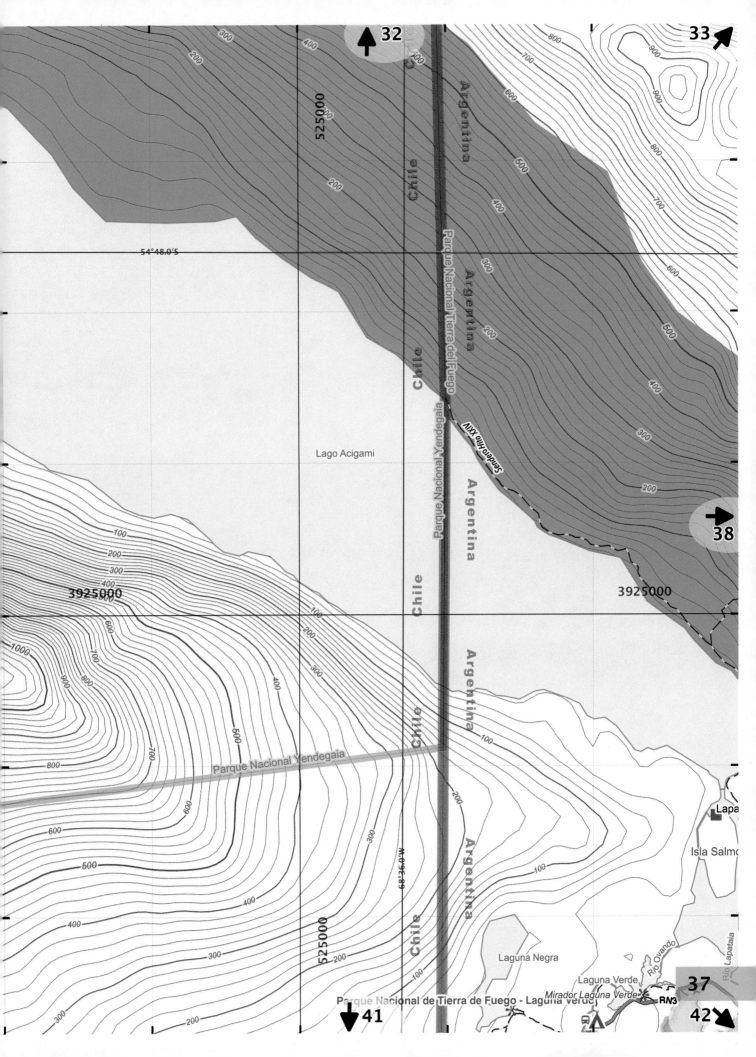

32

33

300
400
-200

800

700

900

800

525000

Chile

Argentina

600

700

500

Parque Nacional Tierra del Fuego

Argentina

400

600

54°48.0'S

Chile

300

Parque Nacional Yendegaia

Argentina

200

Chile

500

Lago Acigami

Sendero Rio XXIV

400

38

300

100

200

Chile

200

300

400

3925000

Argentina

3925000

600

100

1000

Argentina

800

700

900

800

600

200

300

Parque Nacional Yendegaia

Chile

400

600

100

Lapa

Isla Salm

800

300

600

100

Argentina

500

525000

69°36.0'W

300

200

400

Chile

300

200

100

Laguna Negra

37

400

300

200

Laguna Verde

Mirador Laguna Verde

Río Ovando

Río Lapataia

Parque Nacional de Tierra de Fuego - Laguna Verde

RN3

41

42

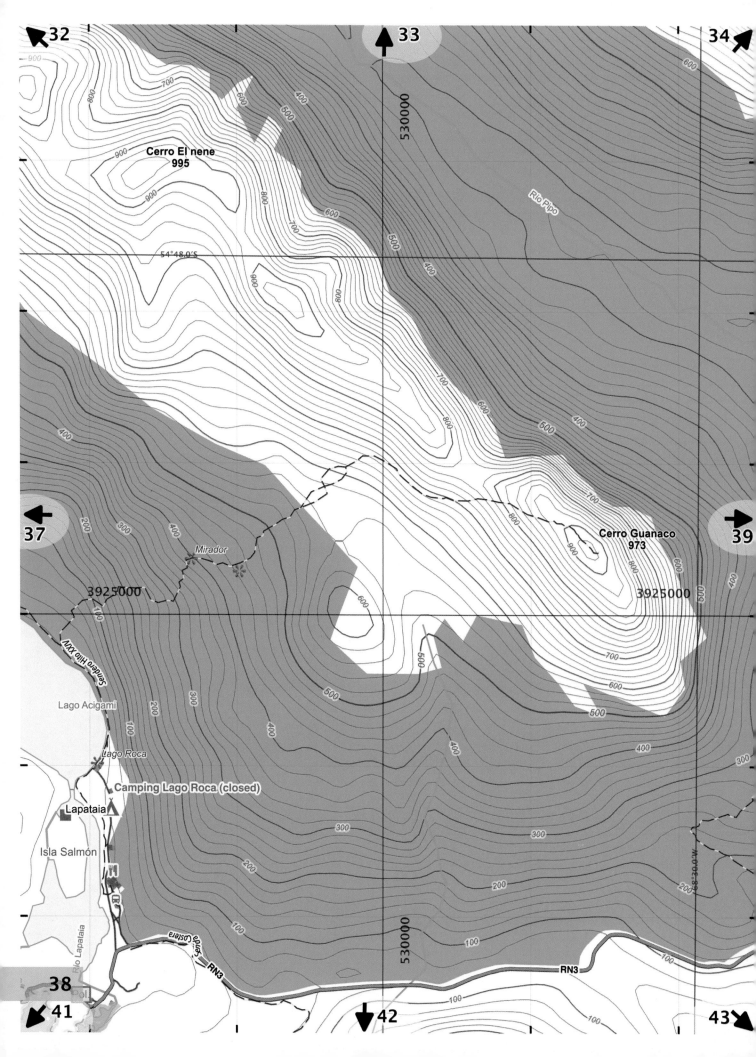

Cerro El nene
995

Río Pipo

54°48.0'S

530000

Mirador

Cerro Guanaco
973

3925000

3925000

Sendero Hito XXIV

Lago Acigami

Lago Roca

Camping Lago Roca (closed)

Lapataia

Isla Salmón

Senda Costera

Río Lapataia

RN3

530000

RN3

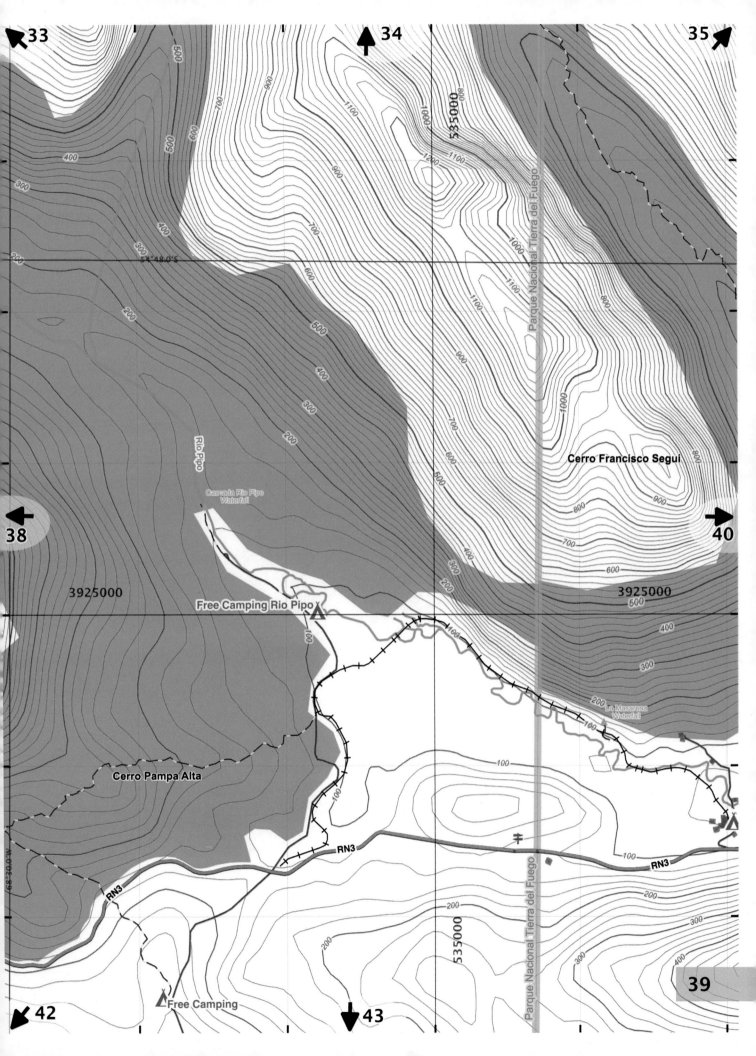

500
900
400
700
535000
300
600
1100
1000
300
1200
1100
400
200
400
300
600
500
400
300
600
500
700
900
200
1000
1100
500
400
Parque Nacional Tierra del Fuego

38

Rio Pipo

Cascada Río Pipo
Waterfall

Cerro Francisco Segui

800
900
800
700
600

40

3925000
3925000
500
400
300

Free Camping Rio Pipo

100
1100
1100

La Macarena
Waterfall
200
100

Cerro Pampa Alta

100
100
100
200

RN3
RN3
535000
535000
RN3

200
200
300
300
400

Parque Nacional Tierra del Fuego

Free Camping

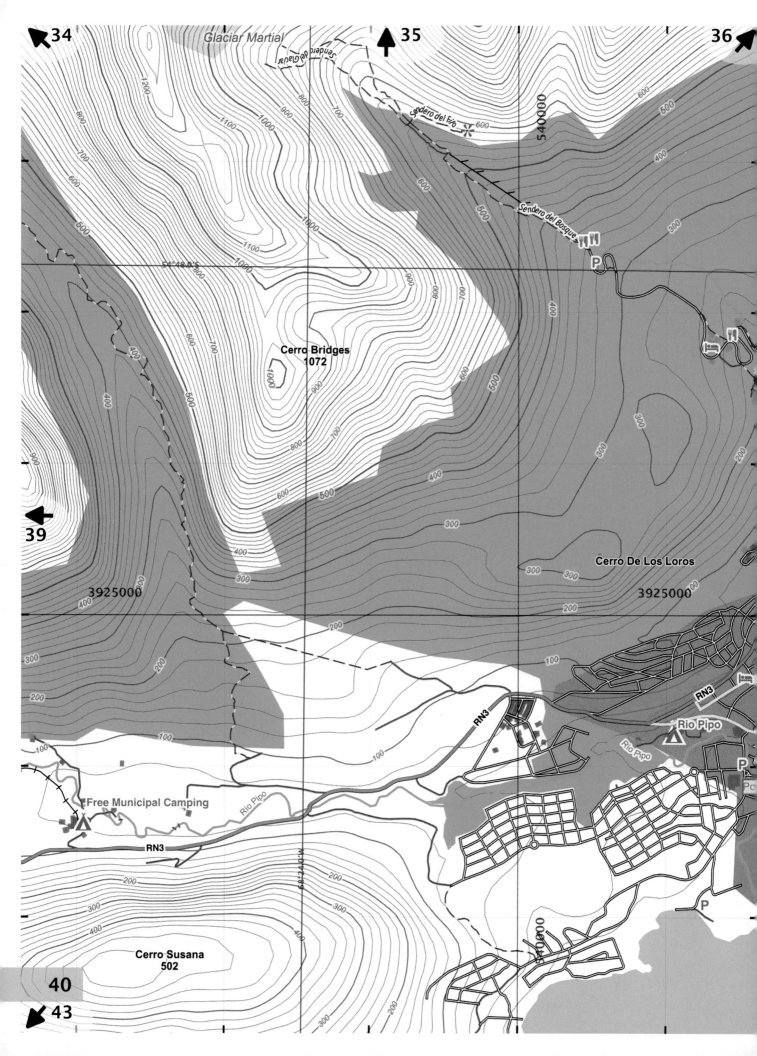

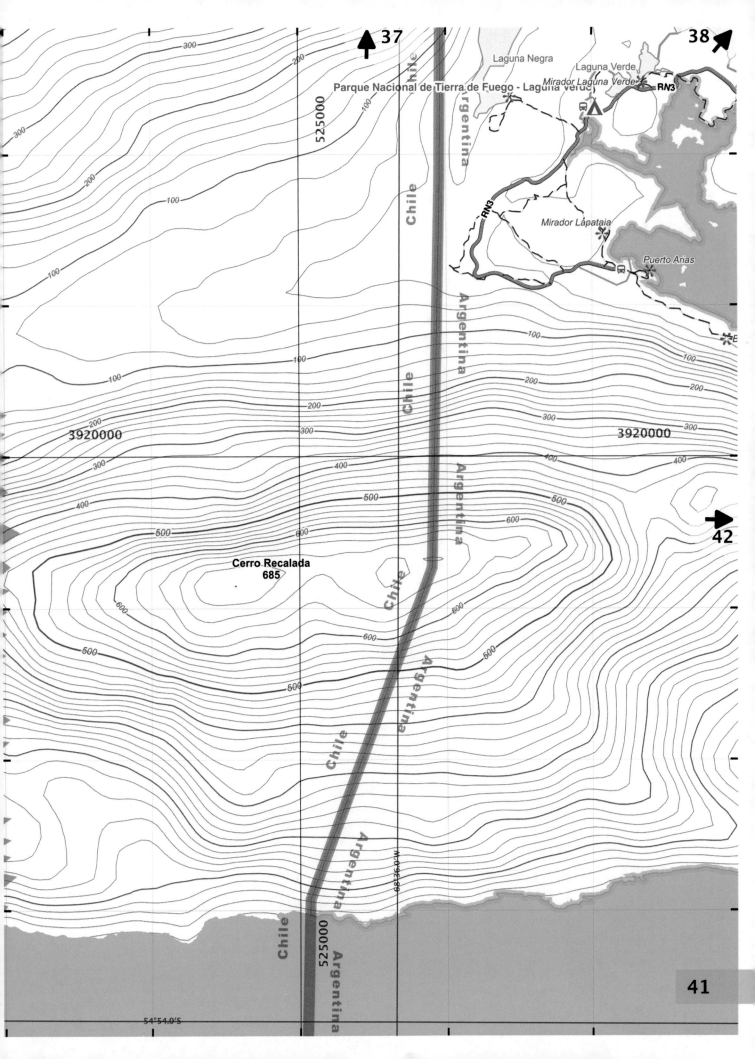

Laguna Negra

Laguna Verde

Parque Nacional de Tierra de Fuego - Laguna Verde

Mirador Laguna Verde

RN3

RN3

Mirador Lapataia

Puerto Arias

300

200

200

100

100

100

100

200

200

300

300

3920000

3920000

400

400

400

500

500

500

600

600

600

600

600

Cerro Recalada
685

500

500

500

Chile

Argentina

Chile

Argentina

Chile

Argentina

54°54.0'S

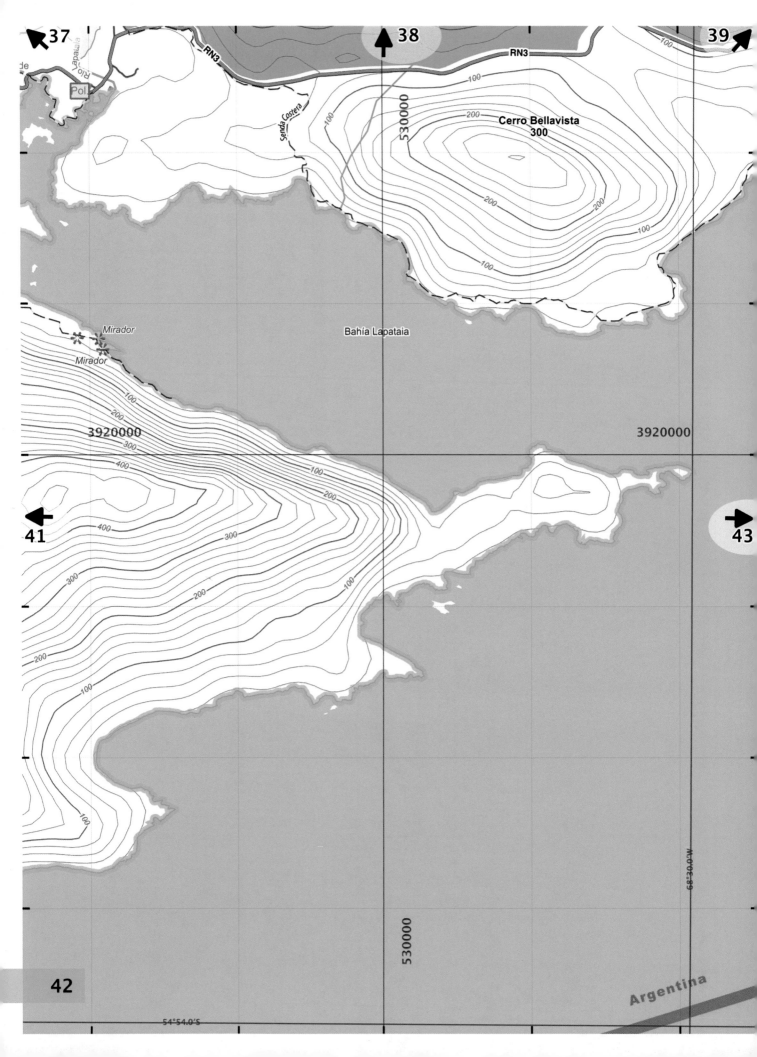

Río Lapataia

Pol

RN3

Senda Costera

100

200

Cerro Bellavista
300

200

200

100

100

100

Mirador

Mirador

Bahía Lapataia

530000

100

200

3920000

3920000

100

200

300

400

400

300

300

200

200

100

100

200

100

43

530000

530000

Argentina

54°54.0'S

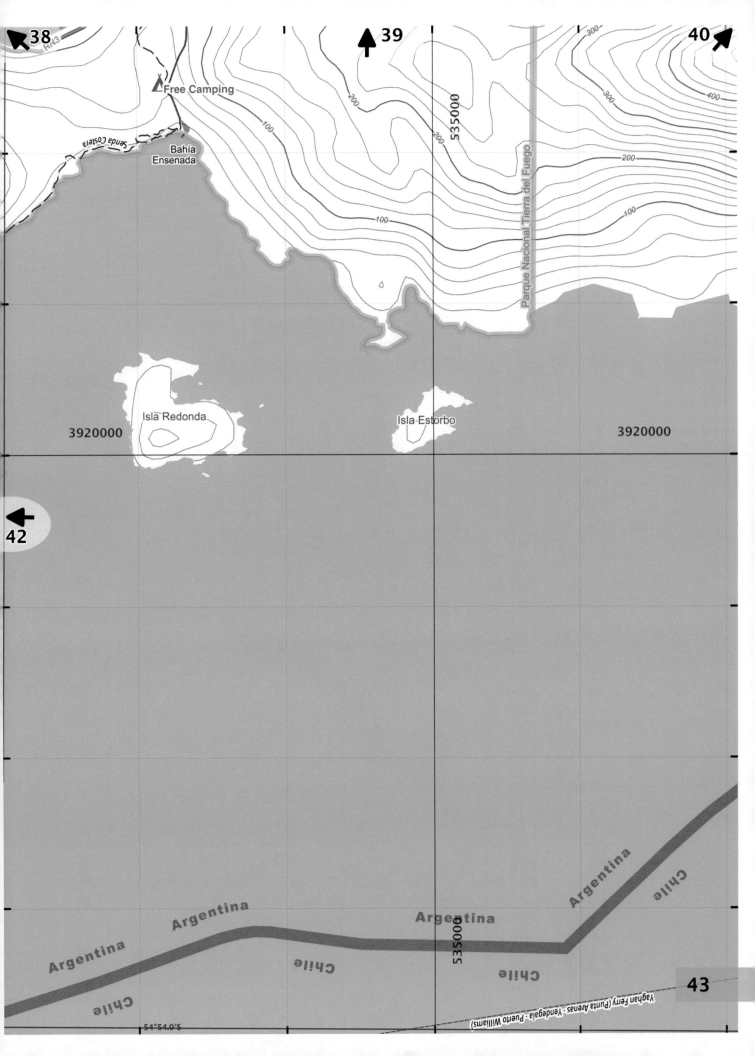

Rn3

✕ Free Camping

Senda Costera

Bahía
Ensenada

Parque Nacional Tierra del Fuego

300

200

535000

200

300

400

200

100

100

100

100

200

Isla Redonda

Isla-Estorbo

3920000

3920000

Argentina

Argentina

Argentina

Argentina

Chile

Chile

Chile

Chile

Chile

535000

535000

Yaghan Ferry (Punta Arenas - Yendegaia - Puerto Williams)

54°54.0'S

Made in the USA
Middletown, DE
14 January 2022

58661492R00027